YOUR KNOWLEDGE HAS VALUE

- We will publish your bachelor's and
  master's thesis, essays and papers

- Your own eBook and book -
  sold worldwide in all relevant shops

- Earn money with each sale

Upload your text at www.GRIN.com
and publish for free

Michael A. Braun

Civil-military cooperation as a vital part in the stabilization-process in Afghanistan

How is its meaning different within certain deployed military actors?

GRIN Verlag

Bibliografische Information der Deutschen Nationalbibliothek:

Die Deutsche Bibliothek verzeichnet diese Publikation in der Deutschen National-
bibliografie; detaillierte bibliografische Daten sind im Internet über http://dnb.d-
nb.de/ abrufbar.

Imprint:

Copyright © 2005 GRIN Verlag GmbH
Druck und Bindung: Books on Demand GmbH, Norderstedt Germany
ISBN: 978-3-640-19019-5

Hauptseminararbeit

Master of Arts in International Relations

Civil-military cooperation as a vital part in the stabilization-process in Afghanistan

How is its meaning different within certain deployed military actors?

Hand in: Thursday, September 22nd, 2005

<u>Student:</u>   Michael A. Braun, BA

Index

Abstract

When policy makers from developed countries gather "to form the world", for a long time military forces were seen as the only ones of impact in areas of war and crisis. They were massively funded and specifically equipped to fulfill their tasks for the best possible outcome. But over the last decades civilian, mostly non-governmental, actors did show up for nation-building as well.

These organizations eventually demanded the right to participate – and than had to deal with urgent reconstruction issues as well. For this the question is how these – civilians and military personnel – work and win "wars" together when they have to. Based on Afghanistan, the paper points on the ever more used concept of civil-military cooperation from the perspective of the military. To gain insight, four different approaches (UN, NATO, US, Germany) are described and explained.

The context of the paper is formed by background-information on the current missions in Afghanistan, Operation Enduring Freedom and International Security Assistance Force. And to get an impression of the cooperation, the paper overlooks the successful Provincial Reconstruction Teams.

The hypothesis of the paper is that successful civil-military cooperation is assumed to be a vital part in the stabilization-process in Afghanistan. This is due to the broad meaning that the different deployed actors put onto it. And, especially the featured military forces / bodies have changed within the last decade.

1 Introduction and academic method

How can two highly different actors – civilians and military personnel – work and win "wars" together when they have to? Based on historical developments and rather new political decisions, the present paper elaborates on this in the case of the reconstruction process in Afghanistan. It points on such serious issue to the global community, since it has been suggested that the lack of cooperation previously was a leading, subconscious cause of failure in military missions.

According to the paper's question, the focus is on civil-military relations in their most often used varieties, which are to be distinguished later. Furthermore the concept is seen as it has been applied massively since 2001 in the Afghan stabilization-process and overall as that it became a vital part of it.[1] The concentration on this specialized reconstruction and development issue is owed to the fact that civil-military cooperation is believed to enhance political stabilization as well.

Also, tasks often cannot be distinguished precisely. Like a medal they mostly have two sides – both, a military and a civilian one. Therefore sometimes the joint management of operations and missions seems adequate.[2] So the question than arises, who can do what best – and than reach the goals together? In the following this cooperation will be described based on it's arise and significance.

Civil-military cooperation is a collective term for all kinds of interactions between civilian organization including individual national and international bodies with the deployed military forces. Both actors normatively seek for co-operation because they than can concentrate on what each could do best rather than fighting trench wars against each other in the same theatre of operation. Moreover, although the media and enterprises do form a massive part of the civilian side, they will not be covered in the paper. Instead the author is concentrating on local, regional and national administrations as well as (international) aid organizations.

The Afghan reconstruction process has been taken as an example because it politically is rather European-led (based on the Bonn framework), whereas Iraq has got a clear Anglo-Saxon branding (US, UK). Therefore it is assumed that in Afghanistan a higher chance for true interaction between the two uneven actors can occur. In the previous perception the military was the last medium to finally solve internal and external conflicts, but civilian actors are, obviously, important for this cooperation, too. However, for practical reasons such as the availability of higher quality research materials, the author has decided to focus on the military side.

Bearing in mind that in Afghanistan some dozens of countries are active in reconstruction, one has limited the investigation to only four (main) players. This is the UN, the NATO, the US and Germany. They all stand for certain perspectives or priorities that are set by their political superior. Some favor a rather civil habit of their forces; others only see the relations with civilian actors as a by-product of what is their real job. Also, the US and Germany are picked because both have got very clear, but different strategies and methodology on the concept and therefore can be used to describe certain ways of thinking towards the topic.

Apart from NATO all actors mentioned are also active (sometimes especially) in non-military missions. Like other civilian and military actors their personnel is deployed based on interna-

---

[1] This statement is also true for the Balkans with regard to the efforts of the Bundeswehr.
[2] Pugh (2001), pp345

tional humanitarian law (e.g. Geneva Convention) and certain national decisions. All want to enforce humanitarian aid and are vital to reconstruction[3]. And as the willingness to intervene solely with military has decreased, more non-military players can be counted. Overall, the UN wants more private bodies doing construction work as well. But unfortunately a general trend can be detected – the environment where humanitarian action takes place is evolving rapidly and poses challenges to the international community.[4] Today's conflicts often are characterized by active, armed and deliberate targeting of civilians, including humanitarian workers, and a widespread abuse of rights. Military actors can secure themselves, but civilian actors depend on the protection by the forces.[5]

But which role do external actors play indeed and how is the meaning of this concept so different amongst them? What are the ideas that are behind the strategies of the deployed actors and why do they behave like they do? Military forces for example are dually present: active as a within Provincial Reconstruction Teams and passive as a partner for civilian actors. The paper is answering these questions for the sake of a broader understanding of the concept and its interdependences.

In the same time this is the hypothesis of the paper: Successful civil-military cooperation is assumed to be a vital part in the stabilization-process in Afghanistan. This is due to the broad meaning that the different deployed actors put onto it. And, especially the featured military forces have changed dramatically with respect to the latter mentioned in the last decade.

For the paper[6] data and literature in books, in particular in periodicals and online sources has been looked at from a skeptical perspective since much can only be estimations. In addition, a lot seems to have been launched or supported by lobbyists from either side. However, it is not surprising that research produces different results depending on affiliation. A useful indication is the findings anyway; whereas they do not provide an answer on the question, they still give indication.

To gain insight on the topic, the outline of the paper is as follows: an introducing distinction between the two actors and their roles will be presented after the introduction. This is followed by an elaboration on the mentioned various concepts of civil-military cooperation. They all involve civilian and military aspects, whereas the line of argument is concentrated on the forces. Also, the German approach is explained slightly more in depth since it later leads to further remarks with reference to the German Provincial Reconstruction Teams. To continue, the currently two missions in Afghanistan, Operation Enduring Freedom and International Security Assistance Force, are described briefly to give some better understanding of the situation. Finally the tactical concept of the formerly US-led Provincial Reconstruction Teams will be explained. This is in preparation of the following remarks on the concept and the conclusion, which ends the essay.

The aim of the paper is to elaborate on the term CIMIC and to present that civil-military cooperation became a vital part in the stabilization-process in Afghanistan. It also seeks to explain how the meaning of civil-military relations differs within certain deployed military actors.

---

[3] Guttieri (2004), p79
[4] Pugh (2001), pp345
[5] Dombrowski (2002), p48 - Therefore non-military actors lean on soldiers for their protection.
[6] Additionally to the paper a presentation was held in the course "State failure, crisis and post-conflict management and reconstruction" on July 12th 2005.

2   Civil-military cooperation – Is this possible?

By common sense, a conflict is the clashing of deferring interests between at least two parties – and they each are determined to pursue their interests and to win the "battle" in the end. Bearing in mind, complex crises arc fundamentally political; they unfortunately often lead to some military actions when states are involved.

Previously, the dynamics of such crisis situations (and especially afterwards) were of the kind that there was only limited need for civil-military interaction and each could exist in isolation. However, the scale and nature of the challenges in contemporary operations are such that no single component can afford anymore not to interact with the other to enable the resolution of the crisis.[7]

Mentioning this, what do civil-military[8] relations mean in fact? There are differing definitions[9] amongst the actors. The military forces argue for it as the military function through which a commander links to national and international civilian actors in the area. This involves e.g. aid groups, the media and local governmental bodies. In addition, under NATO doctrine it is a vital component of the information operations units. The civilian side, however, argues for the "cooperation" usually more as a supportive action from the military forces towards their aims. The assumably common goals of the military forces and active non-governmental organizations might eventually lead to team-work and enhanced communication. Both actors in general do follow for some reasons the international humanitarian law and have the ideas of humanitarian assistance in their minds.

Civil-military cooperation, or CIMIC as some short it, therefore is the broad collective term for all kinds of interaction of civilian organizations and the military forces.[10] This involves "cooperation" as well as "relations" – not only with each other, but also in international politics since they highly rely and lean on them. The concept was developed – and needed – after the radical, global changes of the late 1980s. There was no single body responsible for its development but it rather seems to be a collective understanding and will to do things better than before. And these actions so far were standing for a significant outcome as to be argued.

Nevertheless, military units did not like to exchange information with international and non-governmental organizations, and vice versa.[11] As a result, information sharing has been a frustratingly undone requirement in responses to humanitarian crises. Despite occasional information sharing, this practice has not been sufficiently institutionalized. Thus, collaboration between civilian and military entities cannot be counted on and is difficult to mobilize at the appropriate time.

But by now civil-military cooperation can be seen as a positive connection of two different entities – civilian and military. Both were interacting with each other and acting on the same local scenes.[12] Even more representative would be, however, to argue for civil-military cooperation as the environment within which all relevant actors of post-war reconstruction are op-

---

[7] Spence (2002)

[8] The paper will concentrate only on the cooperation undertaken from a western (North American, European) perspective. It is assumed other regions of importance do carry out other forms of it.

[9] Many of these might not even be called definition, but personal views and opinions.

[10] This includes: own military forces, local (para-) military forces, international military forces, national and regional governmental bodies including public services (e.g. police), national and international non-governmental organizations, and international organizations.

[11] Dombrowski (2002), p49 – And often there is even mistrust amongst the potential partners.

[12] Pugh (2001), pp345

erating.[13] This puts the non-military contribution of the military forces in a broader civilian context and balances it along with the introduction of political and economical actors with humanitarian aims.

2.1 Military component

The military component is only one – though important – element in a contemporary multi-functional, multi-organizational approach to solve a severe crisis.[14] The obvious symbols of strength shown by tanks, jets and other military equipment might be important, but these features often are not enough to bring some form of stable peace and reconstruction into a former zone of crises or even war.

Civil-military cooperation instead works as a force multiplier.[15] So, cooperation can let military leaders prioritize on their tasks, allocate their powers and undertake only appropriate steps. It further could lead to the earliest possible withdraw of forces to allow a return of normality. There are many examples of the commitment to cooperation and information sharing: e.g. the Partnership for Peace and NATO's efforts to improve operations that include civilian and military entities.

The most positive effects of such force-multiplication could be seen in the winter of late 2004. Back than foreign forces were able to show strength in Afghanistan not only military, but also humanitarian. Massive snowfalls and freezing temperatures caused a crisis into which soldiers shipped food, blankets, and cloths. Instead of leaving the population suffering, the idea was that a well-thought approach of how to distribute the aid could support the power of village elders who were loyal to the government in Kabul and friendly to the international troops.[16]

Although the foreign troops had a significant share of the whole operation, civilian elements both national and international were involved, too. In addition, it seems that some deployed soldiers successfully learnt to handle complex, serious situations with local people with flexibility and creativity.[17] They do not act as a soldier, but as humans. This behavior of cooperation amongst helpers and receivers made it far easier for the troops to return back to their main tasks after helping.

What fostered such favorable developments is the current and ongoing transformation of the (Western) military forces. This has for some time solely been interpreted as technological. However, against enemies like the ones in Afghanistan who fight an unconventional war, it seems to be more important to understand their real motivations and cultural background than to gain more high-tech. The money for this might be better spent on improving soldiers' cultural awareness. Technological failures easily can be fixed; human ones not. So, mainly the US seems to have an issue with "great technical equipment, but the wrong enemy".[18]

Therefore, special units to work on the civil-military cooperation were formed to keep this challenge in mind. And since they understand their job as both a function and a capability,

---

[13] Spence (2002)

[14] Echterling (2003), pp32

[15] This means a factor that increases the effectiveness of a military force. Some common force multipliers are new technology, human morale, certain geographical features, weather, and recruitment through diplomacy, training and the pure strength of numbers.

[16] Barnes (2005)

[17] ibid

[18] Scales (2004)

these units really can make a difference. As a result, by now there are soldiers in most NATO armies specifically trained and employed in CIMIC. At the same time, most soldiers on most operations conduct some business for these units in their day to day operations. Though, CIMIC does not have a monopoly on civil-military activities, they are the experts for the topic amongst military forces. This includes providing the commanders with their specific expertise and advice on several CIMIC matters. Therefore the forces transformation goes far beyond a pure technological advance – with good results as well.

For example, by building relationships with officials from non-governmental organizations or local government officials, CIMIC personnel might become aware of a specific (dangerous!) threat to the mission. They have the opportunity to inform the commander, who can send resources to deal with the threat. Rather than having to post patrols on every street corner, the commander's access to information gathered by CIMIC teams has allowed him to employ a smaller number of soldiers, and to use the soldiers he does have available in other crucial areas.

However, the emergence of CIMIC is based in a broader forces development.[19] Information about own, allied and opposing units has always been a key feature. But now the "information-warfare" came up as to describe the use and management of information in seeks of a competitive advantage over the opponent. This may involve the collection of tactical information, assurance that one's own information is valid, spreading of propaganda or disinformation among the enemy.

So "information operations" is the evolving discipline within the military. It has emerged from earlier concepts of the information warfare in the 1990s and mainly US dominated.[20] In this time the military faced completely new phenomena such the "CNN effect", describing the influence of the media on them. Also the enormous advances in information technology made the military pay attention on this field.[21] To a massive degree it now applies to civil-military efforts from pre-crisis situations to post-conflict reconstruction, and spans all levels of involvement.

Though the new technologies have globally arisen and they are widely used, looking at the last war and the ongoing crisis in Afghanistan, one could argue that military forces do face a rather "culture-centric warfare". This is in opposition to the mentioned information- and a network-centric warfare, which some years ago were seen to emerge soon. Therefore the use of conventional CIMIC troops to tackle issues related with deployed forces is of great importance – and growth!

2.2 Civilian component

The other vital part of civil-military cooperation is, obviously, the civilian one. That includes, as mentioned before, actors and institutions such as the diverse field of the media (of a global scale), governmental aid agencies from the country where the crisis occurred and abroad, members or instances of the regional governments and local administrations and uncountable non-governmental organizations along with other international and national actors.

---

[19] Waltz (1998)
[20] ibid
[21] Adams (1998)

This paper recognizes in particular the diversity of the civilian side[22]; especially compared to its highly uniform counterpart such as "the" military (which obviously does not really exist as a unity as well). Therefore one might want to focus a bit more and lead the line of argument towards one or two of these actors. So, the focus will be on the mainly international non-governmental organizations and members or instances of regional governments and local administrations.

The term "non-governmental organization" is globally used in many ways and, depending on the context, can refer to different types of groups or organizations. In its broadest meaning, a non-governmental organization is one that is not directly part of the structure of a government.[23] The phrase is based on certain provisions of the UN Charter about the consultancy work of organizations that are neither governments nor member states to the UN.[24]

Although there have some groups existed before, which also could be regarded as non-governmental organizations, during the 20th century their importance increased dramatically. One of the first such was the International Committee of the Red Cross, being founded in the 19th century. By now this is probably the world's largest group amongst the humanitarian non-governmental organizations. Though voluntary associations of people did exist in history, non-governmental organizations in the current meaning have only developed in the past decades. And now they are a highly heterogeneous group, acting in every field of human interest.

The reason is that some issues in the economy, the society and the environment solely can not be solved within one nation. Also, international treaties and international organizations are seen as being too focused on the developed world. To counterbalance this, many non-governmental organizations try to emphasize on humanitarian issues in general, developmental aid and sustainable development. And in doing so, they decrease their traditionally big distance to the military.[25]

This, however, does distinguish them from the military as an actor in crisis situations. The task for what soldiers are being deployed was indeed usually not to develop countries at the brink of chaos, but to win a battle of whatsoever background. Nevertheless, a battle ends and a war does, too. Than the "survivors" will manage reconstruction and other issues, including the ones, that led to the crisis. Therefore the military bodies become the pioneers for peace as outlined in the UN "Agenda for Peace" [26] – and CIMIC is an integrative part of any modern mission.[27]

For a long time international governments and their forces – either involved during the crisis or not – have left this tasks to local actors like the remaining parts of former governments, the "winner" or non-governmental organizations. Moreover, crises were solved differently, meaning internally due to the bi-polarized world. Nowadays when crisis arise, there is neither guiding nor help anymore. "Failing" states will be treated (and eventually helped) by governments depending on other factors than before. And this also includes the use of the military to stabi-

---

[22] Pugh (2001), pp345

[23] Guttieri (2004), p82

[24] Nevertheless, they all are not a legal entity under international law, like states for example. One exception is the International Committee of the Red Cross which is considered a legal entity under international law, because it is based on the Geneva Convention.

[25] Klingebiel (2004), p55

[26] Liebetanz (1999), pp28

[27] Meyer (1998), p786 – This is true not only for the Bundeswehr as mentioned, but globally.

lize. So, many non-governmental organizations do face a massively increased interaction on "their" original field of action such as humanitarian and developmental aid.[28]

And this is how the civil-military cooperation comes into play. These two actors are now working in the same area – locally and in topic. Therefore there are interdependences as well as there might be positive effects towards each other.[29] So, both could be willing to have a combined planning towards an integrated strategy between responsible military and civilian officials. This is focused on the better use of resources and knowledge on both sides and includes a more efficient application and one, which is according to the individual field of specialization. Nevertheless, the intervention of force is not always to the benefit of the mission.[30]

Bearing this in mind the work of the two actors is obviously different, but based on some kind of the same roots. So, many activities undertaken by either military or civilian actors could be done by the other, too.[31] One big difference, however, is the motivation in the beginning and the time, when the actors start getting active. The private, voluntary US-Aid organization for example does not fight terror in the first place, but provides help for victims not directly involved with the war (combatants) as well as support in cases of natural disasters. Unfortunately a main issue to the civil-military cooperation is a still existing lack of mutual understanding. For this some players take the action and explain what they do.[32]

Therefore, at the beginning of a mission (say reconstruction after the war is over); the typical development non-governmental organization focuses on relief and welfare, which are directly delivered to the beneficiaries.[33] Examples for this are the distribution of food, shelter or medicine, so the activists notice immediately the needs. In a second step they than might foster the locals to start a small-scale, self-reliant local development. And finally the civilian organizations might move away from their operational role, but try to change policies and institutions.

However, the primary purpose of an operational organization in the context of this paper always might be the design and implementation of development-related projects. Whether they are religious or secular does not matter, but many are community-based, public and want to change things to the better on a local scale rather than national or international. And this is the same with the strategic idea why many Western military units are sent into regions of crisis – to change things.

The second civilian actor this paper refers to is members or instances of regional governments and local administrations. They are not charitable and are no non-profit organizations. They instead fulfill tasks assigned to them by their governments. They interact with deployed troops as well, since the local administration has to know about certain actions undertaken by the foreign forces. Depending on the actual case they even might have to be asked by both, the military and the other civilian actors in the field whether they are allowed to perform some actions.

For this, the regional governments and local administrations can be considered as very important for the civil-military cooperation as well. They still or again have authority over their people and are able to lead the "flow of the crowd" in their communities. This includes also to

---

[28] Guttieri (2004), p82
[29] Pugh (2001), pp345
[30] Klingebiel (2004), pp56 – Some non-governmental organizations claim that they were treated differently in Afghanistan after it became public that they work close with the international forces.
[31] Pugh (2001), pp345
[32] Natsios (2005), pp4
[33] Pugh (2001), pp345

help distributing donations and aid as well as to calm down local aggression again the foreign powers interfering their lives.[34]

3 Concepts of civil-military cooperation

As argued before civil-military cooperation is diverse in its appearance and forms. Nevertheless, one thing is clear, cooperation did not happen in the first place because either one actor or the other desperately wanted this. Instead it is far more a partnership to reach common goals than a "love affair" as one might conclude.[35]

Both actors have different duties from different principals or constituents to fulfill. They face some different and some same challenges, but manage them differently. So, the question is which methods, information and data could be shared – or not? And what are the incentives and disincentives of such open policy? Overall there is no doubt that knowledge sharing for the sake of cooperation can massively strengthen trust, transparency, and accountability among the organizations. This behavior, however, is very much dependent on the way how an actor (or participating country) sees itself in regard of their concept of civil-military cooperation. As to be outlined, different actors do have different perspectives on this field.[36]

In the previous chapter the two actors were described rather superficial. Nevertheless, one could see that if they put their strengths together and each concentrates on the tasks one could do best, both might be better off in total. This is also the reason why the military side as well as the civilian one managed to form the Provincial Reconstruction Teams (see chapter 4) recently. They delegate certain tasks and responsibilities back to the actor that has the best track-record on that area.[37] But how did this come and what are the theoretical basics for cooperative actions?

3.1 *Cooperation in practice*

As cooperation means the behavior of people or organizations to work together in common with commonly agreed goals and methods, it is often not easy to reach this state. Either some do not feel appreciated enough, or others even prefer working instead separately in competition. This was the case with many international aid and peace missions in the last decades. The military on one hand did see civilian actors as not equal to them; even a disruptive element. On the other hand for aid workers the military people sometimes really could make things impossible.

Although the need or desire to compete with others, including even pals, is a very common behavior that motivates individuals, it sometimes does not lead to the best outcome possible. So, organizing into a group and cooperate with each other in order to form a stronger competitive force might be what is needed. And this also applies in areas of crisis where civilian and military units are deployed to.

---

[34] Guttieri (2004), p83

[35] Pugh (2001), pp353

[36] Meyer (2004): pp219

[37] This behavior is found widely today including in the business world where it is called the "outsourcing" of tasks that can be performed better by specialized actors from outside the organization.

So, it can be assumed that the mentioned actors faced some cause or mechanism that has forced the cooperation amongst them. From economics one knows experimental results which show, humans often act more cooperatively than self-interest would imply.[38] And this is why it can be argued, the "term" cooperation in civil-military cooperation is meant not only political, but real. The actors might have realized in previous deployments[39] that it is better to co-operate than to defect.

In addition, in this particular case of interaction there seem many conditions met that foster cooperative behavior amongst the two actors. This includes an overlap in desires and needs along with the chance for future meetings with the same organization (and even the same individuals). So, the "memory of the past" and the hope for good future outcomes is seen to provide positive effects to all. In line with this, "quid pro quo" action amongst civil-military work was reported, yet.[40]

3.2 UN approach - Civil-military coordination

The first approach to tackle the issues of civil-military cooperation, the one from the UN, is very specific.[41] Since this organization represents literally the entire world and has nearly every single state as a member, the UN has to take care and be responsible for all of them including taking consideration to all. Their task is to secure peace in the world, support global cooperation as well as economic and social development. In addition they care for human rights and equality of people.

Moreover, this organization clearly executes a hybrid function since it can make its member states, under certain circumstances, sending troops to an area of war or crisis to fulfill tasks of global responsibility as well as it can direct aid units to these places. Therefore the UN is an organization that inherits, though it is by its structure fully civil, both components in it. The military side comes into play with the Security Council; the civilian part from its diverse aid operations. And although they are clearly devoted to peace, military actions can be seen as adequate. This specialty makes the UN unique amongst organizations (knowing that independent states include these functions, too). The other international organizations and national bodies discussed later do focus more on one or the other side.

To ensure the efficient use of military and civil forces for the support of humanitarian operations the UN established a civil-military coordination section in 1995. This section is the interface with the organization towards all governments, international organizations and the military as well as civil defense units when it comes to the use of their assets in humanitarian situations. Than the section coordinates their mobilization as needed and serves as an independent consultant.

Therefore the main task of the section is broad communication, effective coordination and the administrative support in such cases by assigned (from their member states when requested) military and / or civil defense units and structures. This help will come timely, sufficient, and cost-effective to every concerned humanitarian aid agency. The UN's assets include military,

---

[38] Axelrod (1984)

[39] This includes especially the missions in the first half of the 1990s such as in Africa and Asia.

[40] In the case of Afghanistan this means certain commitments from civil agencies were not kept, which in turn led to negative evaluation and decreased trust amongst the military component.

[41] Meyer (2004): pp219 – The UN civil-military coordination and UN civil-military humanitarian coordination are based on the coordination policy (10/2000) and the Oslo Guidelines (05/1994).

civil defense and civil protection units. Therefore the section holds records on their expertise, capacities and range of services which may be offered in case of emergency to member states and multinational organizations for humanitarian disaster relief operations[42].

A specific program[43] ensures that resources are used effectively and appropriate upon availability to respond to humanitarian emergencies of any kind. Also a search and rescue advisory group is available, which could coordinate rescue operations internationally. Therefore this group is consulting some form of military or police task, which now accounts to the civilian component provided by the UN.

In the complex emergencies that happen today ever more, civilians are often directly targeted by violence. The UN civil-military coordination section therefore works to ensure the protection of civilians in armed conflicts and for a greater respect for the international humanitarian law.[44] The section provides leadership in these situations through effective and systematic crisis management. Nevertheless, this does not interfere with any civilian command and control status over military and other assets. While specific military assets remain under military control, the overall mission is under the authority of the UN or a sub-organization.

3.3 NATO approach - Centre of Excellence & CIMIC

Compared to the rather civilian approach of the UN, NATO is clearly focused on the military component of civil-military cooperation.[45] This does not surprise since NATO is the political and military alliance of 26 European and North American nation states. As an international security organization, headquartered in Brussels, Belgium, it aims for the collective and sustainable security of its members.

Since the signage of the North Atlantic Treaty in Washington, DC, on April 4th, 1949 the alliance emerged to be the strongest military one in the world. Moreover, after the collapse of the Warsaw Pact, NATO now unites globally supposingly the largest, most modern and efficient military capabilities and resources.

From the mid-1990s on, primarily in response to lessons learnt in Bosnia and Herzegovina as well as in Kosovo, NATO member states started to develop some broader and more practical ideas of CIMIC on the grounds of liaison with any civilian actor involved in the scene.[46] Having also learnt from the Balkans[47], NATO finally has set up an own doctrine (2001) and even specific staff functions (1998) within any NATO-headquarter as the basic for further engagement.[48]

So the events on the Balkans, which clearly showed the necessity for specialized CIMIC units, triggered NATO. This applies by now for all 'out of area' deployments. As NATO now has to tackle another actual case after the Balkans, the doctrine can be used with the International Security Assistance Force (ISAF) in Afghanistan, which started in 2003 and is so far its biggest mission out of Europe.[49]

---

[42] This includes post war scenarios, crisis situation or environmental and natural catastrophes.
[43] That is the Military and Civil Defense Assets Program.
[44] Meyer (2004): pp219
[45] Jenkins (2003), p128
[46] Pelletier (2004), pp53
[47] Grünebach (1998), pp4
[48] Jenkins (2003), p129
[49] For more information on this please see the actual ISAF chapter later on.

Having said this, NATO has undergone a dramatic transformation in the last 15 years from a defense alliance to an "alliance of mutual interest". In this, CIMIC became an integral part of the spectrum, but its definition went narrower.[50] Is now only seeks for coordination and cooperation amongst the actors and it is purely supportive to assist the military. The key document is the "Allied Joint Publication No 9" (2002).[51] It outlines the three core functions of CIMIC. This are (1) support to the alliance forces from the local population. (2) Civil-military liaison for the coordination and joint planning with civilian agencies in support of the mission. (3) Support to the civil environment by expertise, information, security, infrastructure etc. to the local population in response to their support to the mission. In addition to this the 2001 Military Council doctrine 411/1 is important, too.

In order to establish and maintain the cooperation, NATO has restructured its European CIMIC troops into two main units: CIMIC Group North and South each having functional specialists and general forces. These soldiers will be deployed to support NATO commanders in the achievement of Alliance objects.[52]

Moreover, NATO has planned for the end of 2005 to officially open a "Civil-Military Co-operation Centre of Excellence" (CCOE) in Budel, the Netherlands.[53] The center's idea is to be a multinational institution, which offers expertise and experiences to the alliance-members. This includes education and training for personnel, assistance in further doctrine-development and concepts through experimentation. Participants are the Czech Republic, the Kingdom of Denmark, the Federal Republic of Germany, the Kingdom of the Netherlands, the Kingdom of the Norway, and the Republic of Poland. They all recognize CIMIC as an important tool for their commanders to interact with civilian actors. Their contribution is with military and civilian experts of various backgrounds from governmental and non-governmental institutions, civilian universities and military academies.

Although the CCOE will be accredited as a NATO Centre of Excellence, its capacity and experience is also available to other international organizations like the EU, non-governmental and scientific organizations. The centre is financed and controlled by the sponsor nations and is not part of the NATO command structure.

3.4 US approach – Civil Affairs

Officials in the US only recently have, again, discovered the human component in warfare as well as in post-war reconstruction. After having made some similar experiences in Japan and Germany followed by Korea and Vietnam, Afghanistan and Iraq are on the spot today. The people in charge finally seem to have understood the importance of an adequate policy focusing on the aftermath of war[54], which is designed to avoid post-war instability similar to the one in Iraq today.

Therefore a major directive outlining how military bodies should prepare for future post-war scenarios was given out by the US Department of Defense[55]. Details of it focus especially on

---

[50] Jenkins (2003), pp128
[51] Meyer (2004): pp219
[52] Meyer (2004): pp219
[53] In establishing the CIMIC Groups in 2001, the participants followed political requirements. In 2003 they officially were activated, but it became clear, that a role-shift into a CCOE was needed.
[54] Robinson (2005)
[55] ibid

plans to strengthen the cooperation between military and civilian agencies to plan and carry out essential stability operations together. In addition, the directive aims on the further training of soldiers are in languages and cultural norms. The aim than would be that capable soldiers receive cultural and language instruction to make them a "diplomat" with enough sensitivity and linguistic skills to understand and converse with the ordinary citizen on the street.[56]

A mayor player and input contributor on this is the US Institute of Peace, which was established by Congress as an independent federal institution. Its task is to strengthen the theoretical capabilities of the US to deal with international, political conflicts. In doing so, the Institute develops, transmits, and uses available knowledge on preventing and resolving such conflicts.[57] Based on their common interest in enhancing the effectiveness of civilian-military relations, the Institute and the military improve planning and operational coordination.

Having said this, US forces have maintained Civil Affairs (CA) units including CIMIC[58] since the 1940s; however, they have a broader view and are different to most CIMIC. One reason is the fact, that Homeland Security takes responsibility for internal issues and CA is mostly focused on military, external challenges.[59]

Civil Affairs is the official name for special operations units that conduct civil-military operations outside the US. They are helping commanders by working with civil authorities and the population in the area of operation. Moreover, they seek to lessen the impact of the military during their deployment. With their expertise in civil matters, CA is the principle unit in assisting troops with civil-military operations. To be successful and to achieve the national goals, they contribute by establishing and maintaining networks with civilian leaders. After this, they are also responsible for transforming from military to civilian focus.[60]

US forces also learn much from their allies and enemies;[61] especially the troops that spend some time in foreign cultures bear knowledge. Therefore CA soldiers also act as a liaison between civilians in a disaster area and the home military.[62] They are both informing the local commander of the status of the civilian population as well as assisting in coordinating operations with non-governmental organizations or distributing directly aid and supplies. And once a project has been decided for, CA teams will check the status to make sure the money is spent well.

The majority of personnel come from the US Army Reserve.[63] Their civilian skills allow the reservists to be more knowledgeable and better suited for the restoration of stability and reconstruction than active military. The reservists are gathered mainly of policemen, firemen, doctors, construction engineers, bankers, lawyers, farmers, etc. Therefore the specialists provide some expertise to the host-nation government. They are also able to assess the need for critical infrastructure projects such as roads, clinics, schools, power plants, water treatment facilities, etc.

In addition the "outsiders" (CA) provide the commanders with cultural expertise and keep them informed of protected targets such as schools, churches, hospitals, etc. They also interface with local, international and private volunteer organizations, which provide the com-

---

[56] ibid
[57] USIP
[58] Rollins (2001), p123 - CIMIC is not CA vice versa.
[59] Flavin (2004), ppV
[60] ibid
[61] Scales (2004)
[62] Flavin (2004), ppV
[63] Meyer (2004): pp219

mander with an insight to all civilian activity, ongoing infrastructure projects, and the mission of the organizations in the area. Further more, based on its experiences, CA recognizes the importance of including members of non-governmental organizations in its development activities towards a better understanding of each other's cultures and capabilities.[64] Through these contacts, the actors can improve their cooperation in the field and CA addresses the needs of commanders to consider the entire environment in which their forces operate, especially on local indigenous and international civilian populations.

3.5 German approach – Internal & international cooperation

The second individual military actor discussed in this section is the German Bundeswehr. This is in order to list some different civil-military approaches and to compare them in preparation of the example on Afghanistan presented later.

The German[65] civil-military cooperation procedure is rather integrated. It is somehow broader than in the US, which indirectly separates the national and the international dimensions of the concept due to another administrative body involved. Also the Bundeswehr massively has not only to conduct foreign civil-military cooperation, such as in Afghanistan, but it also could be active in the Federal Republic of Germany.[66] Therefore by law the civil-military relations are maintained in the country and abroad. Based on the "Grundgesetz"[67] the forces are to support policemen, the fire brigade et al in civil defense at certain conditions; and indirectly based on international agreements, German soldiers could serve anywhere. Moreover, with this work they fill a humanitarian vacuum in the area of interest.[68]

Internally the military might be called in case of e.g. a nature-incident. And than there must be some people to be responsible for an efficient communication with administrative, local and medial bodies as well as with the public itself. Moreover in general, every military unit has the responsibility to name "experts" for this task. Nonetheless, there are regional commands ("Verbindungskommando") that guide and lead their subordinates towards the strategy of the higher command.

The task of civil-military cooperation is explicitly described as working with national and international non-governmental and private actors.[69] And as it was until the early 1990s a somehow defense issue, it now has become far more civilian.[70] The Bundeswehr has been told by politics to strengthen its civilian, supportive side. And this is what was done during the last decade. In fact, the distinction to structures such as in the US is the integration and dependability of Bundeswehr units and material for the sake of the public. Currently, Bundeswehr civil-military cooperation can be described as broad and healthy with perspective to develop.[71]

The cooperation in a structure such as the one in Germany does not only rise from just the communication between governmental and non-governmental bodies, but also the – hopefully only theoretical – support in case of a massive incident. This is due to the specialization of the

---

[64] ibid

[65] Along with many other (Western) countries that do not maintain such big forces such as the US.

[66] Meyer (2004), pp219

[67] Namely article 35 on "Zivilschutzaufgaben"

[68] Meyer (2003), pp111

[69] Meyer (2004), pp219 – Teilkonzeption Zivil-militärische Zusammenarbeit der Bundeswehr

[70] Kümmel (2001), p42 – Bundeswehr has undergone dramatic changes in within the last decade.

[71] ibid

military forces on abilities[72] such as pioneering and leadership. This specialization, however, will continue to be expanded more towards current and expected foreign deployments of German soldiers.[73]

Another preparation for both, internal and external civil-military cooperation tasks is the planned (end 2005) CIMIC-Center of the Bundeswehr. This is in spite of the need for more specialized personnel for current and future deployments. The center will educate and house most of the Bundeswehr CIMIC-specialists. They are especially trained in a habit that Germans call "Fingerspitzengefühl" (fingertip sense) to behave adequate in tricky situations either abroad or at home. It also is planned to be working closely with the Center of Excellence mentioned before.

Overall, the German approach on civil-military cooperation is broad and reflects the guidelines set by the political superior. The Bundeswehr recognizes the advantages that come out of cooperation and returns them back to non-military actors.

4   Missions in Afghanistan and the use of CIMIC

Afghanistan has been a turbulent country not only the last decades, but since over 1,000 years. So, due to its strategic location it alternately was governed by Muslim or Mongolian emperors. And even today it is in the interest of foreign powers.

But the "recent" eruptions were the beginning of an even more bloody time. This occurred because of the downfall of King Sahir in 1973. After that the traditionally supporting Soviets started helping in an internal war. This, however, became eventually a proxy war, when the US stepped in for the "enemies". Due to the lack of success on both sides, the Soviets decided to remove their troops in 1988/89 and the "Mudschaheddin" started fighting themselves. At the end the Taliban won, introduced ultra-islamistic rules and controlled 95% of the country.[74]

When the 9/11 terror attacks happened, the US demanded the immediate extradition of the brains of the operation, Osama bin Laden, who was housed in Afghanistan. But, although the international community increased the pressure extremely and NATO declared the collective case for the alliance, Taliban did not hand over their "guest". Instead they were resisting and therefore had to face massive US air strikes for about one month. After that the Taliban regime was defeated.

The year after, the UN Security Council decided for a mandate for the sake of the Afghan country. Now the states community is responsible and seeking for the establishment of security and tries to solve various reconstruction issues. For this, the two main operations will be explained a little more in depth to show the links.

4.1 Operation Enduring Freedom (OEF)

Stepping into the power-vacuum after the Soviet troops withdrew from Afghanistan past their invasion; the Taliban ruled the country from 1996 to 2001. Their extreme interpretation of the Islamic law made them banning music, television, sports, and dancing – enforced by harsh

---

[72] Arbeitsgruppe (2005)
[73] ibid – This includes ABC capacities, mass air transport, and communication.
[74] This was a guess by the end of 2000 according to several sources.

judicial penalties. And it is believed that Saudi dissident Osama bin Laden moved to Afghanistan in 1996 upon their invitation. When they came to power, bin Laden was able to forge an alliance between the Taliban and his al Qaida, which eventually led to a very close connection.

Having mentioned this, latest from 2001 onwards Afghanistan became a pivot for the war on terror. This is also why the US and their alliance partners firstly concentrated so much on this country. Same applies to the Operation Enduring Freedom (OEF), which is now the name of the previous "Operation Infinite Justice".[75]

OEF initially describes the American-led military and intelligence task force for the complete elimination of Taliban and al-Qaida in response to the attacks of 9/11.[76] Along with this, it also is active for the security of certain Arabic waterways. The Operation comprises several subordinate operations in Afghanistan, the Philippines, and especially off the Horn of Africa. However, the term "OEF" typically is connected to the war in Afghanistan, which will be done here as well. By now, OEF also became rather humanitarian assisting than it was planned before.[77]

In the beginning of the operation, the US faced some though challenges with several members of the international aid community due to a lack of communication and cooperation. This, however, decreased over time since civil military operations carried out by CA led to the establishment of greater trust and task-sharing.

It is argued that the differences might have come up because OEF uses the specific US civil military doctrine, which originally was developed for Operation Desert Storm in Iraq and for the Balkans. This includes that any governmental or non-governmental organization always should coordinate with the next available civil military coordination center to make sure that the relief delivered is fine with the forces command.[78] Compared to this, ISAF uses the NATO civil military doctrine developed for Northern Ireland[79] and the Balkans, which is less strict.[80]

4.2 International Security Assistance Force (ISAF)

In addition to the US-led and often maritime acting OEF off Africa, the land-focused International Security Assistance Force (ISAF) is a multinational stabilization force only concerned with Afghanistan. Its troops consist by now of some 20,000 personnel and ISAF is officially mandated due to several resolutions[81] made by the UN Security Council. They basically all want to strengthen the security and stability in Afghanistan, foster the establishment of law and order, introduce human rights to the population along with the promotion of reconstruction.

At the beginning, IASF soldiers were only responsible for securing the capital Kabul and surrounding areas from the Taliban, al Qaida and fractional warlords. This was intended to allow the establishment and security of the Afghan Transitional Administration headed by Hamid

---

[75] To some this phrase sounded like being restricted to the description of the Western God, and it was changed to avoid offence to Muslims.
[76] Falvin (2004), pIX
[77] Falvin (2004), pp17
[78] Flavin (2004), p21
[79] Flavin (2004), p35 - The influence from the UK is due to its initial leadership over ISAF.
[80] Flavin (2004), ppV
[81] These have the numbers 1386, 1413, 1444, 1510, and 1563.

Karzai from end 2001 onwards. But over time, the ISAF mandate and mission were expanded to the whole country. And as both responsibility and the area increased, ISAF now burdens the command over the formerly US-led Provincial reconstruction teams (PRTs) discussed later.

Unfortunately though US troops collapsed the Taliban, the war on terror(ists) is continuing.[82] And the increasing PRT numbers also aim to an improving security and to facilitate the reconstruction process outside Kabul. Moreover, this is necessary if one looks at the millions of refugees and people in the country, who do not have a place to live. They suffer from wars over the last decades and are sick of it.

In order to be successful, ISAF has established a complex concept called "linked up government" with three main areas to be tackled.[83] That is: security, information operations, and civil military operations. Therefore ISAF is far more concentrated on the whole picture and the interactions with every important player in the theater, than the US-led OEF. And this especially applies to all operations carried out, supported or organized by departments of the UN, since close connection.[84]

4.3 Example of cooperation: Germany in Northern Afghanistan

In recent years a new strategy was introduced to Afghanistan by the US. This was to bring the two actors, the civilian and the military ones, closer to be more efficient. Within this concept an administrative unit of aid is formed to be a PRT. Such team usually consists of 50 to more than 1,000 civilians and military specialists that work to conduct reconstruction projects or to provide security for others involved in aid and reconstruction work. Often there are only a few weeks between the arrival of military personnel and civilian actors on the scene of crisis.[85] As argued, the teams were set up by the US to support reconstruction in the provinces. They were led by the US Department of State.[86] Now the teams are backed by specialists from the national and international security forces led by the ISAF.

This includes uncountable infrastructural tasks on a local basis such as the drilling of dwells, the set up of schools and even the pavement of important streets. Moreover, since the PRTs are as close as a foreign organization could get to the local people, they immediately realize the needs. So, further humanitarian aid of supporting organizations can be guided precisely and accurate. For this, in the teams there are typically up to ten percent civilians and the remainder consists of certain military forces. The forces[87] are now directly "supported" by the aid agencies[88], civilian contractors (such as KBR[89]), and civilian police advisors.[90] Also, forces recognize that non-governmental organizations are more flexible in their acting.[91]

---

[82] Rauch (2004), pp16
[83] Flavin (2004), pXII
[84] Flavin (2004), pXIV
[85] Dombrowski (2002), p45
[86] Additionally, the US Departments of Agriculture, Commerce, Health and Human Services, Justice and Transportation had employees working at the teams to assist in their work.
[87] This includes soldiers from CA, force protection, and even intelligence.
[88] Such as the International Red Cross, US-Aid, etc.
[89] KBR is an US engineering and construction company. They conducted much with the US troops during the invasion of Iraq, build the US embassy in Kabul, Afghanistan and erect base camps.
[90] They are responsible for formation / education of local police and the administrative structures.
[91] Pugh (2001), pp345

Having mentioned the functions of the PRTs, the foreign troops play a dual role in Afghanistan: passive as partner for other players and active as PRT provider. One might now want to look on how certain forces tackle the tasks in practice. And since the German CIMIC forces are much respected for their carefulness and diligence,[92] this approach will be looked at en detail: The multinational, German-led Northern Afghan PRTs in Faizabad and Kunduz are mainly focused on the country's reconstruction. In the beginning only little projects were to do for the pioneers, but the tasks became complex and so does the amount of actors involved.[93]

The first German PRT, since end of 2003 in Kunduz, has up to 400 soldiers of which some 3/4 are Germans. The rest is foreign from eleven other countries, which all have recognized civil-military cooperation as a very important element of forces deployment. Only forces might be able to deliver certain results. In fact, many came to help especially because of the good image of the PRTs in terms of sustainable development in former or current crisis regions. And the work itself also strongly can improve the perception, which locals have towards the forces.

Faizabad was opened a year later and has now about half the personnel size of Kunduz. It logistically depends on Kunduz, but has its own structures – and challenges. Faizabad is located in the most important area of poppy seed cultivation. The PRT soldiers are not allowed to do anything against this, but to report to the local police forces. This is also a major issue of civil-military cooperation.

Overall, military the forces are to support the Afghan government, either the local or the national, in securing their influence and a generally stable cohabitation.[94] In doing so, the "networking-experts" leave the camp daily to meet with regional or local dignitaries from state or tribes. There they exchange ideas and plan certain projects, which eventually get more successful because of the personal presence. Also, the joint presence of military police and Afghan police in the streets helps.

The highly demanding component of the tasks is due to the fact that a PRT is a mix of governmental, non-governmental and military bodies, reconstruction of infrastructure and building-up of trust and security. In this particular Bundeswehr case there are also four German ministries[95] involved that hold a stake as well as some non-governmental and private organizations. And finally PRTs also have a military task to perform, which is the assurance of a secure environment to intensify the cooperation of foreign and national aid workers and security forces.

This example shows that in complex emergencies there is no space for competition, but for mutual support and help[96] between the deployed actors. All civilian and military bodies can work together productively as experiences showed proof.[97] Nevertheless, both sides should step back a bit and decide reasonable what is important to them and what can be given up.

On the national level, the existence of a specialized UN section, the development of an independent CIMIC-strategy by NATO and the successful CA-concept in the US made the German Bundeswehr think for an own concept. To have something like this became especially

---

[92] Grünebach (1998), p18
[93] Rauch (2004), pp16
[94] Rauch (2004), pp16
[95] This are: Ministry of Defense, Foreign Ministry, State department, and Development Ministry.
[96] Giller (2002), p614
[97] Kobe (2001), p10

urgent after the incidents on the Balkans, where the Germans were highly active. But the ideas that were to be introduced were different to other forces and organizations.[98] Germany has gone a specific way between forces and military, between national and international tasks.

4.4 Remarks on CIMIC based on this paper

After the collapse of the bipolar world in the end of the 1980s, the military faced new enemies and tasks. It also had to cope with an ever increasing number of civilian actors in their original field of work – and vice versa. This is why the military came into a far closer relationship with civilian actors and organizations.

As outlined it is not easy to find a clear explanation to the term civil-military cooperation / CIMIC since different actors put different meanings on it. This behavior created rather confusion, than some collective understanding. Also the differentiation between the different tasks (E.g. which organization is doing which tasks in civil-military cooperation?) is very difficult. But one thing is clear; CIMIC is not only simple, naïve "building of houses and dwells" by soldiers, but the honest and effective contribution from military forces to international missions in order to gain security and development.[99] These forces work as the hinge between civilian organizations and the military. And the troops have proofed to be an active, major and vital part of any modern peace building mission. [100]

Since all of the military (and civilian) actors mentioned above operate in the same area, they did learn much from each other. They are all part of missions with the same goal. But the work with these organizations could be organized better, more effective and more open, especially from the perspective of the military forces.[101]

There are some common principles to any member of a civil-military relationship. This is: (1) cultural awareness (the actors must acquire knowledge of local culture, customs and laws), (2) common goals shared by forces and civilian actors must be established and recognized (this is the basis of cooperation), (3) shared responsibility for a better goal orientation within each role (to avoid misunderstandings and inefficient work), (4) consent, (5) transparency in aid related topics in order to support the common goal and enhance the cooperation (successful missions require mutual trust), and (6) clear, true communication.

The most recent military operations have shown that relationships between the military and civilian forces exist at all levels and in many different contexts.[102] Therefore the actors must be able to work in cooperation with any governmental, international and non-governmental organization. CIMIC provides the essential link between the deployed actors and is the liaison to support the forces and the civilian environment. The concept can contribute to an enhancement of mutual understanding between military and civilian actors.[103] The analysis shows that close civil-military consultations at all levels are beneficial to the mission's goal.

But overall, it is understood that civil-military cooperation will be successful in the long run.[104] The sometimes undertaken distinction of CIMIC from other civil-military relations

---

[98] Braunstein (2000b), pp23
[99] Braunstein (2000a), pp47
[100] ibid
[101] Grünebach (1998), p18
[102] Rehse (2004), pp15
[103] ibid
[104] Jenkins (2003), pp128

shows that e.g. NATO is following a narrow description and that they see it as a troop-supporting factor. Compared to this the German Bundeswehr has a rather broad definition. And so does the US, if one accepts the whole concept as one piece including the parts that are done by Homeland Security.

Military support for the implementation of civilian tasks within the reconstruction process has to be conducted to civilian bodies.[105] Although the military in general is mandated and controlled by politicians and therefore their people, a non-governmental organization seems to be even more people- and issue-led than forces ever could be. Further more, some countries, organizations or alliances might even use their military presence in certain areas for political and economical reasons. But this is not what they should do. These actors should work accordingly to their task descriptions and not for the sake of some national aims.

In strictly humanitarian terms after withdrawing from the scene the indigenous population shall be left at least with some peace and stability. Obviously the assessment of security, development and stability will be carried out in the long term by international organizations and non-governmental organization in close cooperation with the local population. Until this happens the military is in charge according to the terms of deployment. So in short term, CIMIC personnel must be ready to fulfill these tasks the best they can. And as soon as specialized organizations arrive they have to make sure, that cooperation and teamwork is done good.

5   Conclusion

Based on recent developments and political decisions, the paper elaborated on civil-military cooperation at the case of the reconstruction process in Afghanistan. It has pointed out how civilian and military actors effectively work together, although they are different by many reasons. To gain insight, four approaches (UN, NATO, US, and Germany) were introduced and explained. And the paper's context was formed by the two missions in Afghanistan, OEF and ISAF. Moreover, to check cooperation in practice, one overlooked the German PRTs in Afghanistan.

As stated in the introduction, the hypothesis of the paper was that healthy and successful civil-military cooperation is assumed to have become a vital part in the stabilization-process in Afghanistan. Now, this is regarded as proofed due to the broad and effective meaning that the different deployed actors put onto it. According to the paper's question, the focus was on civil-military relations between military forces and local, regional and national administrations and aid organizations.

To conclude some final implications and outlooks might be of help: CIMIC is believed to enhance stabilization, but "lines of demarcation" between the actors shout for a review. Although previous crisis led to cooperation, there still is a need for an intelligent redistribution of tasks; everyone should do what they can do best (capacity, capability). There is also a need to discover hidden resources and appropriate requirements to further stabilize the region in question. This comprehensive approach does not mean that the military shall control the civilian actors in post-war reconstruction or vice versa, but that all recognize each other.[106] It would lead to a more effective reach of the presumed common goals. And to achieve it, they

---

[105] Rehse (2004), pp17
[106] Spence (2005)

will have to communicate more. This will range from basic communication even to the sharing of strategic planning and analysis.

In addition political guidance for civil-military cooperation has to be developed[107] and lessons learnt from previous deployments should be revised meaning adapted. This leads to better preparation, less disruption and more efficient procedures with focus on the importance of CIMIC. Furthermore, one can argue there should be "marketing" to ensure this in the minds of senior military staff. Moreover, all potential non-military players need to know how to talk to the relevant soldiers. Sometimes they want to cooperate, but do not know how to address the forces.[108] And finally commanders and politicians should think about providing training for non-military reconstruction workers. An example for task-oriented education by the forces could be the training classes provided for journalists by the Bundeswehr in Hammelburg, Germany. These classes prepare them for the most possible scenarios they might discover when going to crisis areas for their work.

Regardless a long and extensive development-period, the concept and methods of civil-military cooperation is not yet at the target.[109] Instead, the two actors need to develop further and make each other more embedded in the area of their operations and structures. So, although a positive result can be stated, one still might find the vital need for a professional moderation of all actors involved.[110] This task perfectly could be undertaken by a recognized international body such as the UN.

---

[107] Flavin (2004), ppXV
[108] Flavin (2004), pp73
[109] Rollins (2001), p129
[110] Haas (2002), p310

6   List of references

Adams (1998): Adams, J., *The next world war: Computer are the weapons and the front line is everywhere*, Simon & Schuster, New York City, 1998

Arbeitsgruppe (2005): Arbeitsgruppe „Unterstützung durch die Bundeswehr im Katastrophenschutz der Länder" des Bundesministeriums des Innern, des Bundesministeriums der Verteidigung und der Länder Bayern, Nordrhein-Westfalen, Thüringen vom 20.Januar 2005, *Lageeinschätzung,* Gemeinsamer Bericht, Berlin 2005

Axelrod (1984): Axelrod, R., *The Evolution of Cooperation*, Basic Books, New York City 1984

Barnes (2005): Barnes, J., *When banter beats bullets*, US News & World Report, US news section, volume 138, issue 8, p21-22, 07.03.05, [Academic Search Premier 07/12/05]

Braunstein (2000a): Braunstein, P., *CIMIC 2000 – Zivil-militärische Kooperation*, Europäische Sicherheit, Gesellschaft für Wehr- und Sicherheitspolitik, Jahrgang 49, Mittler, Bonn, p47 - 50

Braunstein (2000b): Braunstein, P., *Spezialisten und Generalisten – CIMIC 2000: Zivil-militärische Zusammenarbeit im erweiterten Aufgabenspektrum*, Truppenpraxis/Wehrausbildung, Jahrgang 44, p23 – 28

Dombrowski (2002): Dombrowski, K., *Militärische und zivile Komponenten in Post Conflict Peace-buliding-Missionen – Die Schwachstelle der internationalen Gemeinschaft?*, Österreichische Militärzeitung, Jahrgang 40, Bundesministerium für Landesverteidigung, p45 – 50

Echterling (2003): Echterling, J., *CIMIC – Zivil-militärische Zusammenarbeit der Bundeswehr im Ausland*, Europäische Sicherheit, Gesellschaft für Wehr- und Sicherheitspolitik, Jahrgang 52, Mittler, Bonn, p32 - 37

Flavin (2004): Flavin, W., *Civil Military Operations: Afghanistan – Observations on civil military operations during the first year of Operation Enduring Freedom*, US Army Peace Keeping and Stability Operations Institute, US Army War College, Washington 2004 [Academic Search Premier 07/12/05]

Giller (2002): Giller, J., *Zusammenarbeit zwischen Militär und NGOs: Von Vorurteilen und Pragmatismus zur Symbiose?*, Österreichische Militärzeitung, Jahrgang 45, Bundesministerium für Landesverteidigung, p609 - 614

Grünebach (1998): Grünebach, H.-P. *Im CIMIC-Einsatz beim Hauptquartier SFOR, Sarajevo, Bosnien-Herzegowina, 24. März bis 24. September 1998, Eindrücke – Begegnungen – Folgerungen*, Streitkräfteamt Abeilung III, Fachinformationszentrum der Bundeswehr, Bonn 1998

Guttieri (2004): Guttierei, K., *Civil-military relations in peacebuilding*, Sicherheitspolitik und Friedensforschung, 22. Jahrgang, 2/04, Nomos Verlag, Baden-Baden 2004

Haas (2002): Hass, F., *Das Konzept der interlocking institutions – Realität oder Chimäre im Einsatz? Dargestellt am Beispiel der Zivil-Militärischen Zusammenarbeit in Bosnien und Herzegowina*, in: Biermann, R., Deutsche Konfliktbewältigung auf dem Balkan – Erfolge und Lehren aus dem Einsatz, 1. Auflage, Schriften des Center for European Integration Studies, Nomos, Baden-Baden 2002

Jenkins (2003): Jenkins, L., *A CIMIC contribution to assessing progress in peace support operations*, International Peacekeeping, autumn 2003, vol. 10, issue 3, p121-136, [Academic Search Premier 07/12/05]

Klingebiel (2004): Klingebiel, S., / Roeder, K., *Eine neue Allianz? Das Verhältnis der Entwicklungspolitik wird enger*, in: Weidenfeld, W., Internationale Politik, issue 11/12, Deutsche Gesellschaft für Außenpolitik, Berlin 2004

Kobe (2001): Kobe, R., *Entwicklung und Perspektiven des deutschen CIMIC-Einsatzes*, Notfallvorsorge, Jahrgang 31, p6 - 10

Kümmel (2001), Kümmel, G., *Civil-Military Relations in Germany: Past, Present and Future*, SOWI-Arbeitspapier Nr. 131, Sozialwissenschaftliches Institut der Bundeswehr, Strausberg 2001

Liebetanz (1999): Liebetanz, K., *Zivil-militärische Zusammenarbeit im Ausland (CIMIC) – Keine Eintagsfliege*, Notfallvorsorge, Jahrgang 29, p28 – 32

Meyer (1998): Meyer, Ch., *Ein Modell für die Zukunft – Deutsche CIMIC in Bosnien*, Truppenpraxis/Wehrausbildung, Jahrgang 42, p782 – 786

Meyer (2003): Meyer, Ch., *CIMIC-Konzeption der Bundeswehr*, CIMIC Faktoren I: Militärische Aspekte, Speyerer Arbeitsheft Nr. 155, Deutsche Hochschule für Verwaltungswissenschaften Speyer, Speyer 2003

Meyer (2004): Meyer, Ch., / Vogt, M. (ed.), *CIMIC-Faktoren*, Speyerer Arbeitsheft Nr. 159, Deutsche Hochschule für Verwaltungswissenschaften Speyer, Speyer 2004

Natsios (2005): Natsios, A., *The nine principles of reconstruction and development*, Parameters, US Army War College, Autumn2005, vol. 35, issue 3, pp4-20, [Academic Search Premier 07/12/05]

Pelletier (2004): Pelletier, J.-J., *The role of CIMIC within NATO operations*, Polaris Quarterly, Autumn 2004, vol 1, issue 3, NATO School, Oberammergau 2004

Pugh (2001): Pugh, M., *The challenge of civil-military relations in international peace operations*, Disasters, reader in international relations, University of Plymouth, issue 25, Plymouth 2001

Rauch (2004): Rauch, A., *Sind neue Strategien für Afghanistan nötig?*, Europäische Sicherheit, Gesellschaft für Wehr- und Sicherheitspolitik, Jahrgang 53, Mittler, Bonn, p16 - 20

Rehse (2004): Rehse, P., *CIMIC: Concepts, Definitions, Practice*, Hamburger Beiträge zur Friedensforschung und Sicherheitspolitik, Institut für Friedensforschung und Sicherheitspolitik der UHH, Heft 136, Hamburg 2004

Robinson (2005): Robinson, L., *When fighting ends*, US News & World Report, US news section, volume 138, issue 20, p36, 30.05.05, [Academic Search Premier 07/12/05]

Rollins (2001): Rollins, J.W., *Civil-Military Cooperation (CIMIC) in Crisis Response Operations: The Implications for NATO*, International Peacekeeping, volume 8, no 1, Spring 2001, Frank Cass Press, London 2001

Scales (2004): Scales Jr., R., *Culture-centric warfare*, Proceedings, US Naval Institute, issue 10/04, vol 130, p32-36, [Academic Search Premier 07/12/05]

Spence (2002): Spence, N., *Civil-Military Cooperation in Complex Emergencies: More than a Field Application*, International Peacekeeping, Spring 2002, volume 9, issue 1, p165-172, [Academic Search Premier 07/12/05]

USIP (n.a.): The United States Institute of Peace, *The Institutes Mission* [Internet - http://www.usip.org 07/12/05]

Waltz (1998): Waltz, E., *Information warfare principles and operations*, Artech House, Norwood 1998